The "IT Factor" of a 6 Figure Stylist:
Get more clients and skyrocket your income

For more information and learning tools, visit the website iamsharonsmith.com.

Printed in the United States of America

First printing July 2016

ISBN-978-1-365-15930-5

THE "IT FACTOR" OF A SIX FIGURE STYLIST

Chapters

The "IT Factor" of a 6 Figure Stylist

Learn to earn with the secrets to the good life.

Learn to Win, Win, Win

You wake up, get dressed, and head out to work. After you fight the traffic to the salon, you give yourself that pep talk in the car about how this day is going to be different and you're going to make it BIG only to walk in for another day of boring haircuts, mediocre tips, and annoying coworkers. You thought that you would do more with color, cuts, and fashion, but...no. What happened? No overflowing money and bills are due. A little while later kids come along. Then it's schoolwork, homework, your work, your spouse's work, the house work... All of this work but still no money. Life kicked in at full gear and you got stuck in the rat race that is life. It seems like everybody is moving forward but you.

So then you began to analyze your life for the problem. So you look at....the salon. Let's take a look around... There's always a leader of the pack in every salon. They are usually polished and wearing the latest in fashion, electronics, and cars. They got the perfect teeth, hair always perfect, and they smell delightful. Well... they should because they make enough! You may think to yourself. Their prices are so much higher than yours. You're still wearing last year's fashions or maybe even a few years before that because you have responsibilities unlike theirs. You are responsible. You have packed a lunch because heavens forbid you spend too much. You're still trying to keep your prepaid phone on and who has time for a carwash .You're doing good to be insured. They never miss their lunch hour while you work straight through yours because you're just happy to be busy at that time. That stylist can have people waiting and they seem to just wait; but you, No Way! Your clients are grumpy and looking for another chair to grace until you can get your act together because they have another appointment and never mind that they were late for yours.

So you run and rush trying to please them and it seems they demand more and more and then they're gone in about 3 months and you're left with a time slot open on your book. Hustle time again! But how? There has to be a better way. You stand by and watch that main stylist while every other stylist in the salon is doing an act of worship or envying, trying to be like that person or steal their business right from under their nose and it just can't be done. Every person that walks through the door wants to sit in 'THAT' chair. Why, because that stylist has "IT". The style God has blessed them with all things good. You know that they are just a mediocre stylist, nothing fancy but every person that walks through the door seems to love sitting in that chair. It's nerve wrecking and seems a bit unfair. How did they get the "IT" factor? What is it about that person that makes them different? You are a better stylist, cutter, and all around, just better. You've tried to be nicer than nice. You've given services away for free. You have bent over backwards, short of walking their dog, but the clients still have no sense of loyalty to you. Why? How can you be the one with the "IT" factor? It's time to learn. It's time for you to take control and live the life you want. It's time for you to be what YOU want to be. The IT Factor is going to be you. You are about to learn to Win, Win, Win.

1. Set your mind for the "IT Factor"

Learn to Win

There is a better way. This book will share things that are helpful, things that are positive, and can help to build you up as well as teach you how to run yourself like a business. You will learn how to change. You are the architect of your moment and the time is now. Where you are, I have been, so I know it is possible to change. I will talk about what can make you a better person or at the very least make you look at what you do differently. This book is designed to help you reprogram your brain and attitude. This will require work on your part, but if you take the time to read this book then a little work is not a problem. The principles that you will learn will empower you and make you want to be better than you ever thought. This book will not only make you a better stylist but a better person. It will empower you in your personal life as well as your business life. It will improve your self esteem and your outlook on life. You will now embark on a journey of self discovery and awareness that will make you more positive and more beautiful inside and out. This is the journey that I took and I learned so much about myself and my world. I changed everything about my life for my benefit and I have never looked or longed for the things behind. I am thankful to God for this discovery and I now share that outlook with you. Steps are laid out for you and will be easy for you to follow. Take time to read them slowly and keep a journal so you can look back and see your changes. Each chapter will start with affirmations and stories as well as end with an exercise that will help build you up and help to clear your thinking. Now I want you to stand in your reality. The one YOU make.

...You got to learn to hate losing so bad that it makes you a winner...

-ET, The Hiphop Preacher

Realization

I knew this girl from my childhood. I was a year older than she was. She always had this big dream for herself. It seemed all would be lost when she got pregnant, dropped out of school and got married... in that order. Her husband was abusive and everything looked like a dead end. I just knew this was the end of her life, but she still had these big dreams... really? I would think to myself, " This is truly the highlight of your life", but deep down inside of me, I admired her. I never would have admitted that back then. I knew back then that she was different. In fact she was so different that she nearly convinced me that she was born rich and I knew she was barely upper poor class. I watched her and ya know what? She became just what she wanted or thought herself to be. Why? Because she was already there in her reality! The lesson I learned is this: Reality is whatever you decide it will be.

Realize that you have the power to change everything. You have the right, contrary to what you may have been told, to be whatever YOU choose to be. It doesn't matter what happened in your past- that's over. Living in the past has the same effect as cleaning out your refrigerator and throwing out all the rotting and decaying food that you forgot was in there only to put it all back.

Would you want to go back to the trashcan and pull it out to look at it yet another time? No, because you can't change its spoiled state and it just stinks. Living in the past does nothing for your future but stink it up. You also can't change it. If there is a lesson to learn, learn it and move on. I was reading my Facebook page one day and someone posted this proverb:

If you are depressed, you are living in the past.
If you are anxious, you are living in the future.
If you are at peace, you are living in the
present.
-Lao Tzu

Be careful where you spend your mind because it will affect your emotions. Live in the moment and prepare for your future. Never become a wanderer with your life. A wanderer is a person who never makes plans. They just go with the flow and they dream a lot rather than make a plan. This is the person who dreams of the lottery. They like name brand clothes but have no savings account of any kind. If this is you, the step is to recognize it and then you *can* change. Don't hide it from yourself because then you set yourself up for everybody knowing you're crazy but you. Make goals and commit to them. We will discuss more about that later, but write it out so that you become the planner of your reality. Your reality is whatever you want it to be. If you allow others to define your reality, they will and you won't like how they do it so take control of that for yourself and be what YOU want to be. All things begin and end with **you**. Your life. Your reality.

This is where you may have to clean your friends list so to speak. There are some that don't want you to change and some that will stand in your way by keeping you comfortable in your old ways. These are the ones that don't necessarily fight you about change but they keep bringing up the past, like spoiled food. The past is gone, period and you can't live there so let's move forward. Concentrate on a fabulous future. Your future success is not limited by a lack of "Know how" or lack of resources nor is it governed by past inabilities. Get rid of the person in your life who has never succeeded at anything but always want to tell you how to make your life better .... Huh?! It could be your Mom. You can't get rid of Mom, but you can do Mom type things with her, but do not share your realities with her. This applies to any person who wants to stand in the path of your future. There are also people that just like to offer negativity to you like they are serving a dish with your name on it as if it's *for your own good*. These types of persons are what we call haters, gossipers, negative talkers, jealous family members, naysayers, revengeful Exes, and even some of your coworkers and bosses present or former. These people are completely NON-FACTORS to you. A Non-Factor is any person that has nothing positive to add to your life and your new reality should be protected from them. Close your mind to them. Don't entertain them, as a matter of fact; dismiss them right out of your life. Don't waste an attitude with them or on them because they are just simply not worth the extra effort. You can use that energy on bettering yourself and your craft. The non-factors will become your cheerleaders later because they are going to want to benefit from your limelight... They always do. Smile and walk away.

Think about what you want to be in every detail. Write it down in your journal and read it often. Feel that feeling until it feels real. This will become a part of your motivating factor. This will make your reality come to life and this will make you live and be alive your reality.

Your reality is your seed of motivation so keep it safe. Commit to your reality and make it live.

"Nothing ever becomes real 'til it is experienced."
— John Keats

Personal Commitment

I have a saying with my kids. "Do it. Don't half-ass it." Yes, I said ass... moving on. Nothing is more nerve wrecking to a parent than to have a child do something half way. My parenting style is you will do it until you do it right and that worked for me. I had all day to sit and watch you do it. You need to have that same attitude with yourself. Success always starts in the mind. **Decide that you are going to be successful and commit to it**. Get some motivational CDs like Les brown, Zig Ziglar, Jim Rohn, or Dennis Waitley to name a few and it's so many more. When you begin your journey of change you won't have a lot of support especially if you're coming from a negative environment. You need to hear as much positive talk as possible. One thing I do is play CDs rather than listen to the radio. Commit to yourself for a better self. This was my beginning of changing my mindset and at first I didn't even know that's what I was doing until it began to happen. I became more positive. I began to see different ways to do things. I noticed some of my friends were not very positive or encouraging. I became thankful for small things and I shared more of myself. This is how you should start your day or end it. Ideas will come to you during this process and you will flourish this way. You will start to see yourself and things or people differently. This is needed because during your transformation, you will need to stay positive and if those around you are not changing right now, you will have to take this journey alone for a while. Take charge of success. Learn about it. You will find friends who are moving in the direction you're taking. Like will notice like and your new world will begin to unfold. Do daily affirmations. This is crucial to your becoming successful. The more you do it and the more you meditate on the affirmation, it will begin to cement your reality. It will feel strange at first because it may not be true right now. One thing that help me with affirmations is saying it in a way that my mind could accept it. I was out one morning doing my daily walk and I was listening to Hal Alrod's podcast and I don' remember the exact episode but the person he was talking to or maybe it was him.... Either way, he mentioned about saying affirmations in a "I am dedicated to....." format rather than stating it like you are already there because the brain knows the truth and you don't want it fighting with you to stand in its truth. You want it to change. So, if you state it in a way that the brain can accept the brain will make it happen because it will look at it as something you're accomplishing and not as a lie. This worked wonders for me and I began to excel at a much faster rate. You will too.

Remember this you are making it real so keep it up. I know you've heard the saying "Fake it until you make it". This is true. Anything you want to be has to be faked first and then the habit is formed. Only those who are broke and intend to stay broke want to keep it real. Faking becomes real if you do it long enough. We will discuss more on the "Keeping it Real" type of thinking later.

You owe it to yourself to commit to success. We as humans become creators of habits or comforts. Make a promise to yourself that you will step outside what feels comfortable and do something you may not like to do. It's for your good. Do it till it feels right, then, do it some more. You have heard the saying; Birds of a feather flock together. Think of the people you are around most often. It's common knowledge that you will be like who you are around the most. That is how cultures are formed. If 5 of your friends are broke, fat, or negative, you will be #6. Let's narrow this down.

Name the first 3. Now, think of their habits. Do they think like you? Are they where you are striving to be? Do they help you think and plan for the future or are they just wondering through life and using you as company? I'm not asking you to dump your friends, but merely to expand your horizon. All people are created with the seeds of greatness within them so you are not better than the next being, but every person may not be good for your vision. Find people that think or do the things you would like to do and develop their mindset. You are doing this for you and tell yourself that every day. As you go along you will notice that your circle of friends will change and most of all you didn't have to get a 'stank attitude' with no one.

Set goals for yourself and don't be afraid to write them down. With each goal that you write down, write out the steps needed to reach that goal. Goals are a lot like preparing a recipe, especially baking. Baking has to be very precise to have the desired results. Write out your goals just like you would a recipe and follow your plan. Pace yourself so that you don't get burned out or feel discouraged. The important point here is that you are doing it. Remember the Hare and the Tortoise. Consistency is what counts. It's not how fast you get there but the fact that you will arrive. This is a journey that will teach you so much about yourself, your circle, and your journey in itself. I will say that in the beginning it will feel strange, but you will learn so much and grow to heights you've never imagined. If you hang in there and when you look back, you will see your growth and laugh a wonderful laugh, wondering how did you ever get stuck there. Understanding is key and it's delightful.

Strategize

Starting out I felt like I could just have goals in my head. I didn't want to write them down because I didn't want them to fall into the wrong hands. That was my fear until I realize I had to stand in my own reality. This goes back to the **NON-FACTORS**. Let me clarify who Non-Factors are. They are people who may have a lot to say about what you do, who you see, and how you get things done, but they offer no funding or moral support. They pay for absolutely nothing. They may also offer their opinion on your life as if you need it but don't get sidetracked with their opinions because their opinions don't matter. They may just be haters who want to see you fail so they will have something to talk about. I'm warning you beforehand to not give them any of you time. I was giving too much of myself to them like I didn't want them to feel bad. You have to develop some tough skin here and let others perceive whatever they choose. They are **NOT** paying any of your bills so *Poof* be gone with them. Writing goals down is the key. I can't stress that enough. My dreams did not take shape until I took them out of my head and put them on paper. Putting it out on paper gives your goals a life of their own so that they can impact yours. The goals began to live for you rather than just being dreams in your head. This is where strategies and affirmations work hand in hand. Make it a habit of looking at your goals daily along with your affirmations. Positive thinking is also a key factor. Sounds crazy but it works better than negative thinking ever could.

With each goal that you write down, write out the steps needed to reach that goal. If you don't know the steps, that's okay. Write it down anyway and the steps will come to you as you look at it each day. It will motivate your brain to think in ways you never thought possible. The grandest gift you have is your brain. If you challenge your brain to new heights, it will not disappoint you. The brain will always rise to the occasion in a magnificent way. Exercise your brain with puzzles. Read something daily. Keep a journal. Listen to motivational CDs and picture yourself being where you want to be. Feel that feeling and it will be your reality. Pace yourself so that you don't get burned out or feel discouraged.

You got to be Hungry...
- Les Brown

Be Hungry For Change

You know what physical hunger feels like, but do you know what hunger for change feels like? Physical hunger can make you feel sick if it's not satisfied. Being hungry for change can do the same thing. That sickness that you feel is your mind and body's way of telling you that you deserve better. Your brains way of saying; challenge me. Look around at everything around you. You may be working harder rather than smarter.   When you're hungry for change, it means you recognize the need to want change. This is a place in you when you realize that staying the same hurts more than the change. YOU GOT TO WANT IT. That is being hungry for change but change requires work.

Change won't happen just because you said so and it's not always easy. If it were, we wouldn't have people addicted to drugs, drinking alcohol, food, and the like. Since it's easier said than done, you are going to have to find a reason to change. Give that some thought so you can find your 'Why'. It may be family, or you desire financial freedom, or maybe you just want to be better. There really has to be a reason or a motivating factor for change. As stated take some time and look for a reason or factor that will help you in your transformation because if there is not one, you won't commit to change. It's human nature to look for and want to be comfortable. If you're comfortable, then you're not growing so step out a little bit. We do what is comfortable automatically because it's familiar to us and it's makes us feel safe but remember that feeling is short lived when you're struggling for money. Right now in this moment you have to choose: Do you want to be comfortable now or very comfortable later? You have to learn the skill of 'delayed gratification'. Delayed gratification is planning out your goal and achieving it by following a definite plan of action. That skill will serve you so very well if you learn to wait and plan. Trust me on that one. Just do it. It will make you rich, both physically and emotionally. It makes you harness your skills and you will no longer work for a paycheck but for the big game at the end. Change starts in the mind first so meditate on changing until it becomes a hunger. Hunger comes when you get tired of losing. Want it, feel it, and be it. Remember not everyone is going to be happy for you but you will be happy for yourself in the long run.

Story about a dog

An old farmer had a dog. The dog was rather lazy but all in all a really good dog. One day after a day of lying in the sun with his master, they decided to have some porch time with the neighbor. Well as the dog began to lay down, one of the boards was loose and he slipped and fell off the porch on to that board. A nail that was imbedded in the board pierced the dog on his hind leg. He yelped and cried but never got off the nail. The neighbor being agitated ask the farmer why is that he didn't help his dog. The farmer watched the dog but never moved and he said if it hurt bad enough, he would move.

That dog is like a lot of people. They groan and complain but never change. Change takes commitment. Be willing to do it for you.

Here's my story...

I wasn't the popular girl. I didn't make the best of grades nor did I care like I should. I just wanted to get through it and be done. I didn't want to stand out too much so I would try and blend into the background. I was a nice person just trying to slide by but I wasn't getting by. I became a hairstylist where I thought I was going to make all of this money and I was barely making ends meet. I got married and had kids but the struggle was still real. I began to drive a school bus and work in the salon but the getting up at 4 in the morning, traveling 25+ miles to my first pick up, with my kids in tow was just too much. I was so broke that I decided to go back to school for something in the medical field. That was a waste of time because when I finished all I had was a ton of student loans and no job. With bills piling up and kids growing up I lost everything I had. No house, no car, and no job. I took the small amount of money I had and opened a salon but I didn't know what I was doing and therefore lost all of that, too. It was during that time I noticed that there was no help for a stylist or the help that was available was more than $10,000.00! Hello... If I had that kind of money I wouldn't need your help so badly! I was so broke and desperate but I knew if I could get some help I could do better. Every hair show I attended was teaching all of the practical stuff and I fell for that too. If I could only roll hair better, or do the super weaves, romantic updos, curl, flip, color... It goes on and on and on. I have taken so many classes and bought so many kits, colors, products all in the name of doing better and making a better living and I got it all... somewhere. I knew it had to be more to it than what I was getting. There had to be a business side to all of this. I started making changes in how I did things and it began to pay off in a big way. The first thing I did was read and read and read some more. That's when I discovered that running your salon business is a lot like running any other business. It's not just you; it's YOU as your business. The minute I began to do that, I began to notice big changes in my business as well as in my personality and personal life. I took some time to write down my rules for my business and that became the basis for my business. I no longer became every client's best friend. I thought I had to make every person like me so I can make money but that is simply not true. I stopped targeting every person but I fine-tuned what it is that I am good at and focused on that. I am happier now and I make the money that I need without having to stress about every penny. I have come up with this guide so that you can bypass the hurt and began from day one making a good and decent living or if you've been in the business for a while, take your business to another level and be brave enough to make the money you desire. I'm an average person with fears just like you, so if I can do it, you can too; and you will be glad you did.

2. Setting up your "IT" Factor" Business

This is where life gets exciting and your creativeness takes hold. Here is where you have to open your mind to the goodness and strength of dreaming and dreaming big. If you can dream you can create but make sure you're coming from a good place. Work is required for this leg of the journey more so then anywhere else so be mentally ready. This is also a very important step in setting up and establishing your business from the development of your vision and your mission.

"If you can see it in your mind, you can hold it
in your hand".
- Steve Harvey

What's your vision and mission?

You need focus of your mind to clearly understand your direction. Your vision is your ultimate, overall goal of what you would like to achieve. Your mission is how you plan to accomplish your vision. This is like the map that's going to take you in your desired direction. On this map make sure you plan to have some stops to pick up key players for your vision. That would be partners or investors, mentors, employees, and definitely customers. You can also acquire attorneys, bankers and the like.

The Plan- Salon Training 101

The plan should always be in writing. Invest in a notepad of some kind that can hold all of your thoughts and plans during your process. The plan is written so that every person that it concerns can be on the same page and have a clear understanding of your vision. It needs to be plain and simple to understand so that confusion is kept to a minimum. This is the time to also decide what type of structure you want. Here is an overall view of each. The Pros and cons are not labeled because what I consider a pro may be a con for you, depending on your situation and circumstances.

Sole Proprietorship-

- It's the simplest of all because there is only one owner. YOU

- The business doesn't have to be registered with the Secretary of State

- The owner takes all profits and losses

- There is no asset protection and you are responsible for the business expenses

- The business is taxed at an individual tax rate

- You are considered self employed

- You own your **JOB**, not a business

General Partnership-

- Two or more owners

- The profits are split between all owners

- Each partner shares the responsibility for debts and claims against the business

- No personal asset protection

- The business doesn't have to be registered with the Secretary of State

- Each partner pays self employment tax for profits received from the business

- You own your **JOB** with others

Limited Partnership-

- Have to file with the Secretary of state

- Have at least one general partner and one limited partner-can be silent

- One partner can run the entire operation on a daily basis

- Limited partner may contribute funds but may or may not work in business

- Limited partners have no personal liability for the business' debts

- All owners pay taxes at their individual tax rate

Limited Liability Company-

- Known as an LLC

- Must register with the Secretary of State and pay filing fees

- Have Articles of Organization on file with the Secretary of State

- Owners are called members

- Owners have limited liability for business' debts and claims

- Owners can choose to be taxed at a cooperate rate or individual rate

S-Corporation-

- Articles of Incorporation must be filed with the Secretary of State and corporate filing fees paid

- Owners are called shareholders

- Income passes through to owners

- Shareholders have limited liability from business debts and claims

- Profits and losses passes through to the shareholders

- The business must file an information return and taxes are paid by individual shareholders on individual tax return

C-Corporation-

- Articles of Incorporation must be filed with the Secretary of State and corporate filing fees paid

- Owners are called shareholders

- A board of directors manages the business. In most states this can be one person

- The business can stand alone on its own with its debts and liabilities

- The business must file its own tax return, separate from your personal tax return

- An annual meeting is required by law and must be documented

This is a very condensed look at the different entities, but there is a lot more to it. I would suggest you look into it further to gather more information so you can pick the one that best fits your needs.

Business License, Bank Account and Tax ID Number

After you have taken your state's board exam that is required to be a professional, you need to now invest in a business license and a tax ID number so you can get the benefits of being self-employed. You will want to register your name and your business because it will make you eligible to take certain tax write offs. To maximize your benefit you will need to open a business account for all of your business expenses and earnings. A business account is a good way to keep up with all of your profits as well as losses and at the end of the year it will make doing your taxes so much easier. Get use to business terminology so that you can better access and understand your bottom line. Here are a few words that you should become familiar with and begin to use and understand.

- Business Plan- Even the simplest of operations needs to have this. It will keep you focused and on track with your goals and your business will have shape and you will be more than just someone who does hair.

- Exit Strategy- You have to start your career with the end in mind. Where do you want to be in 1, 5, 10, 20 years. I know a lot of people don't like to think about it, but we age every day and you have to decide how do you want to retire and plan for that. I would hate for you to reach retirement age and have nothing to retire on or maybe you would like to retire early and pursue other interests. The time to plan for that is now.

- Marketing Strategy- How are you going to advertise your business and how are you going to track what works and what doesn't? Marketing is a big art of your budget so you want to plan and execute it well so as to maximize your return on investment.

- Budget- This is your fixed cost and your adjustable cost. Fixed cost is what you have to spend out regardless of what you make. This would include your rent, phone cost, supplies, and the like. Your adjustable cost are the things that change in price like your utilities, certain supplies, gas in your car, mileage and the like.

- Goals- Your goals should be designed to get you to the next stop on your business plan. Goals help you to focus yourself and center your activity so keep going like you are following a road map. Never forget goals. They are your markers to success.

- Business Income- Know your bottom lines. This is your business income. You should know how much your business is spending so you will know when your business profit begins. You need to know what every client costs you down to the penny so you will know when you have made a profit.

- Profit and Loss- Without this you will never know if your prices are too cheap and you could be giving away the kitchen sink. A profit/loss statement is needed so you will know when you can have a sale and what is your bottom line or lowest price you can run a sale without redlining.

- Reconciliation- Helps you keep up with your bottom line. This can be done on a monthly, quarterly, or yearly schedule.

Keep a binder with all of this information available to you. It's good to compare months so you will have a good road map of your success. You will be successful if you have a plan and you following it.

A Summary

All of this goes into your plan which is just an extension of your vision and mission. This is the detail version of that. This is a part of your road map. Your map must contain your itinerary which is all your stops and plans for the trip. Cover all of the things that could hinder or slow your plans like; what if you don't open or staff on time? What if income doesn't come as soon as you thought? Can you keep up with marketing and planning? These are just a few questions. There are so many more that you can think up and write down so as to avoid certain pitfalls. Take some time to get this done. I know this is not the part that can be appealing but it's essential to your success. Spend at least 15-20 minutes a day on your dreams and that way you won't get overwhelmed and you can enjoy this part of the process. Keep your eyes and ears open and pick up ideas that you like from different sources like books, magazines, people, and mentors. Gather ideas and make a scrapbook of the things you like. You also want to crunch some numbers so you can present your plan to banks, partners, private investors, or even relatives or friends that can invest. Having your plans down in writing and organized shows that you're serious and ready for another level in your life. Have a checklist of key things needed in your vision. Some of the things you should have on your checklist are:

- Company goal and plans for the future

- Description of the business and a statement of what you do

- What type of ownership you plan to use

- Summarize your management and daily operations

- Keep a company diary with your business history in it (This is your business "baby book" so to speak)

- Describe your services and products used or made

- Take a look at your competition and strategize by analyzing your market

- Plan your marketing strategies and consistency

- Plan your employees and their job description

- Project income for the next 3-5 years

- Know your expected income and expenses for the month and for the year

- Remember your licensing fees, resale ID number for retailing

Communication and Bookkeeping

Communication is key to your success because this is how we are reached and how we communicate to the world. Always make your mission clear so that those that hear it know how you can help them. In communication should be:

- Your business cards
- Facebook, Twitter, Instagram, Periscope
- Your website
- Online booking
- Email communication
- Your telephone number
- YouTube

Your bookkeeping is very important so you will always know where you stand and if your goals are being met. Depending on your personal needs this can be done daily, weekly, or monthly. I personally prefer weekly, over monthly. This helps me to see potential problems and fix it beforehand. Things that can help you with your bookkeeping are:

- Online booking

- Quickbooks

- A Certified public accountant

- A ledger for manual input

- Your bank

A credit card terminal is good to have so you can eliminate checks. A good alternatives for a terminal are Paypal, Swipely, Square Up, or Intuit. They all charge a nominal fee for their services and no monthly cost is incurred for equipment. Opening an account with any of them is relatively easy.

Finding a location that fits your needs

You need to decide if you want to work in someone else's salon as a commission person or booth renter or open a mini salon like a salon suite or your own salon. Location is key to the niche that you are targeting.

Commission pro and cons:

- Works for a salon or person
- Your time is theirs, like a job
- You may have to wear a uniform
- You're not responsible for anything but your space and tools
- You may have health insurance and vacation time
- Salon usually does the marketing
- Work like a team with other stylist

Booth renters' pros and cons:

- You're free to set your own schedule
- You're responsible for your own marketing
- You have to pay rent even if you didn't work
- You are responsible for your own products and tools

- You set your own style and rules for your business

- You can easily become "your job" if you fail to plan

- Get paid daily

Mini salon/suite pros and cons

- You're free to set your own schedule

- You're responsible for your own marketing

- You have to pay rent even if you didn't work

- You are free to set your own schedule

- You're responsible for your own marketing

- You are responsible for your own products and tools

- You set your own style and rules for your business

- You can easily become your job if you fail to plan

- Get paid daily

- You have privacy and security of your own space

- You can have more than you in your suite

- You can decorate however you like

- Requires license and whatever fees for a small business

- Sky is the limit

Full salon pros and cons

- You're free to set your own schedule

- You're responsible for your own marketing

- You have to pay rent even if you didn't work

- You are free to set your own schedule

- You're responsible for your own marketing

- You have to pay rent even if you didn't work

- You are responsible for your own products and tools

- You set your own style and rules for your business

- You can easily become your job if you fail to plan

- Get paid daily

- You have privacy and security of your own space

- You can have more than you in your salon

- You can decorate however you like

- Requires license and whatever fees for a small business

- Sky is the limit

No matter which you choose you can make a good living at all of them. You have to decide which one you like better. With a suite, it could be an office of your choosing or a place designated for such. Buying equipment can be nominal if you're willing to do some work like Ebay or Craig's list. They are good sources for buying at really good prices. Small beginnings are just as good as big. Your professionalism is what counts.

AFFIRMATION: I am dedicated to running a successful business

I am dedicated to listening to myself so that I can live my dreams. I will review my plans daily so I know for sure I am on track. I will be successful and positive and I will enjoy my success and money. I deserve it. I will dismiss all doubt and fear and I have no worries. I will stay faithful to my plans right down to the end, and I will finish and be satisfied with myself and my plans because this is my time.

3. Get the "IT Factor" look

Get the "IT FACTOR" look

Imagine you need a lawyer and you look through your local directory or maybe you get a referral from a friend. You call him up and set up an appointment. You arrive early so as not to waste his time and you find out he's not there. You sit down to wait when finally the lawyer wanders in through the door. He's dressed in sweat pants with a dress shirt and tie. The shirt needs ironing, he's wearing sneakers and his hair is uncombed. He invites you back into the office. As you look around the office, you notice a lot of dust. Books and papers are everywhere and the office is painted fuchsia. You sit down to tell him your problem. The lawyer looks around for a pad so he can write down your story but he can't find one so he decides to write your case down on the back of a receipt he found on the desk. What is the likelihood that you would want to hire this lawyer? If you did, you would be considered just as crazy as he is on some level.

This type of scenario happens every day in some salons. A client can walk in well before the stylist gets to work or coming back from lunch, errands, and the like. The stylist knows nothing about the client or even what time they came in. The stylist looks like they just got up out of bed or just left the gym to come to work. The salon walls are in some of the loudest colors known to man. There are broken chairs, broken equipment, stained towels, and over all uncleanness throughout the salon. Nothing is in place and a lot of time is wasted looking for things that should have been cleaned and tucked away in its place. Things are missing that are needed to complete the service for the client so the stylist has to improvise and just all around fly by the seat of their pants and hope the client's hair turns out well. Some salons can make Sha-nay-nay from the old Martin shows appear like the genius of hair and class and that's for real. I will stop right there because it's enough of the negatives. This is a recipe for broke and struggling forever. This is how we get burned out in one of the most productive/lucrative fields in the world. Right now in this chapter, we are just trying to get the look and everything else will be addressed in the proceeding chapters.

The Salon

The look is everything around you. If the salon has a less than stellar look, it is time for you to find another salon or upgrade your act if you're an owner or booth renter. I'm not saying things have to be new but they have to be clean and neat with no tears, rips, or too faded. Keep it as fresh as possible. All state board rules and regulations must be followed. Make sure your work area is clean. Be careful with the use of bold colors. You don't want to overwhelm the client with colors that are too dark or can glow in the dark without any help from you. Bold accent walls are okay and are a good expression of your style and personality but not on every wall in the salon. Keep most walls neutral. Neutrals do not have to be beige or brown. They can be colored, but just a really soft hue of whatever color you choose and one or two accent walls for drama. Put your own personal artwork on the walls. Don't put up posters of products and hair that you didn't do. Those walls are very expensive and they should be working for you. Use plug-ins or oils with a soft clean smell all around the salon to set the mood from the client's entry, but be mindful of allergies so stick with soft scents. The décor needs to be pleasing to the eye or professionally done so as to merit top dollars. Clients buy more than just you when they walk in the salon. Take the time to get up any hair or product off the floor before you start your next client. It shows respect for your craft and for the client. No one likes to go to a dirty bathroom and if your station is full of the DNA of your previous client it will have the same connotation. Have enough capes so that you can use a clean one for shampooing clients each time. It's good to have cloth capes for styling. Always use a neck strip (I use sani-towels that I break in half; they are a little more cushy) with your shampoo capes for sanitary reasons and it adds more value to your service and it's a value that the client can see. If you are one to get clients wet, then double cape to keep the client dry. Purchase the smaller or child cape and put them on backwards before draping with the larger one. Client robes are always a good investment if you have a place for them to change. You will need to provide and area or laundry bag for the client's use while they are being serviced. Be careful with this because you can become responsible for their belongings if you don't have a safe place for their things. If you use the laundry bag method, the client can keep up with it themselves but if you have a responsible person who can keep up with this, it will add extra value to your service because the client can truly relax and enjoy your environment.

This is all for the comfort of the client and shows that you care. Everything that is done in the salon is to set a mood for a pleasurable visit. Coffee or teas are always good options to offer. Serve them in real mugs or tea cups and have small cookies or pastries on hand served on small dishes as well. Real dishes can be cumbersome but it is a touch that adds value. If you can't invest in real dishes then a good paper products will work. It is better to have something rather than nothing. This will set you apart from your competition and puts you in a category by yourself so that your prices are your prices. The clients are investing in a feeling and that feeling has to be a good one or they will be hard to keep. If the client stays with you in less than a stellar environment puts you in the position where you may start to discount the price of your services to keep them longer, or they may like you as a person, or you are more than super good so that they tolerate you just until they find what they need somewhere else. Some clients will leave you anyway because they are total price shoppers and they go from salon to salon. That is not the client you're going for. That client is not your ideal client and you don't want your entire clientele model based off of this kind of client unless you want to live with anxiety and less pay... just saying.

Prices

Post your prices or have several hand held versions of your prices. The handheld version will be called your price menu. Put your clients at ease with knowing the base prices of your services. During your consultation is when you should give the client a rundown of their service cost. The price menu will take the guest work out of pricing and puts the control back in your hands and does not make it seem like you just made up prices from the top of your head. Giving your clients full disclosure builds trust and people love doing business with people they trust.

Bathrooms

Advertisement doesn't stop just because nature calls. The bathroom is only the beginning of tantalizing the senses. This is where you can put homemade soaps, lotions, and air fresheners that can't be found everywhere or anywhere else. Put shelf talkers in the bathroom so that the clients will know you have that product for purchase as well. Shelf talkers are small signs that tell information. You can print them on your computer and place them is different areas of your space to tell about specials, tips, or whatever you would like someone to know. I love shelf talkers. I place them on decorative holders and place them throughout my space so my clients will know I have gift cards, I sell jewelry and whatever else. Another good idea is to have a liquid soap or have the solid soaps cut into small thin slivers that can be used up in one hand washing. You can make a display of the full size bars that can be glued inside of a cake plate with a dome for display and placed/glued in a safe spot on a table or shelf. Look for your local product makers. Make your own scent and make it a salon exclusive. You will have to contract this and negotiate your exclusive scent. You can become a seller for someone local that can supply you with the products and you make sure you have them for purchase. Make sure it is something that is plentiful and unique. If it's a fragrance or a product that is discontinued it has to be taken out of the bathroom and placed on clearance. The bathroom is prime real estate for full priced items only. This is good for you and the wholesaler that you use. Make sure it's someone reliable and love what they do so that product is available to you on a consistent basis. It's a good idea to have your own private label placed on it so as to have the product available only through you. Make that a part of your contract with the wholesaler. If the radio can't be heard in the bathroom, this is where you would want to place one out of reach and inconspicuous to the clients. Here in the bathroom is a good place to just run ads with soft music playing in the background. It sounds like a hard sell but it's really not as long as you make it informative and not sells pitchy. It's information and clients love information.

Clocks

This is something I learned well into my career from one of my mentors. I came from a very small salon with a lot of older ladies who had been in the business for years. They didn't charge much but really they couldn't because it was one of the most unprofessional places I had ever worked in but I didn't know it at the time. When I decided to leave and go to a more upscale place I stuck out like a sore thumb. As I unpacked my things I had a clock. I thought I was contributing to the salon because as I looked around, there were no clocks. My mentor quickly schooled me about that and I had never realized until that moment that that clock was one of the sources of my anxiety. This has become so much a part of the salon experience that this subject of clocks requires a subheading of its very own. You are going for a posh experience and to complete the experience, clocks are not a part of your décor. Never put visible clocks in your salon. The waiting area of a salon will become just like the waiting area of a doctors' office when a clock is added. Just think of yourself and the things that cross your mind when you're sitting in a doctor's office. I know for me 'Hurry up' is always playing. Keep the time on your station or in areas that is visible only to you and other co-workers. There are some clients who are time watchers and this can interrupt the salon experience and that makes for nervousness for you and for the client as well as other clients who are within earshot. If you are asked the time, kindly share it with discretion, but don't stress yourself with clock watchers. What is a clock watcher? They are generally clients that hate to wait. A five minute wait seems like five hours to them. They usually don't tip or tip in very small amounts but they demand top notch service. They may come in every few months, or for a period of weeks but nothing significant. This type of client can wreak havoc on a salon environment. Let them use their cell phone to tell the time if need be so at least you won't have the stress of knowing it. **NO VISIBLE CLOCKS!**

TVs, Computers, and Radios

Be mindful of the volume as well as the content. It is best to pipe in music or purchase CDs that are more neutral, like a soft jazz, pop, soft rock, or nature sounds and have it play on loop. The best thing to do is make your own CDs that you can place your own commercials throughout. This will require quite a few CDs if you run monthly specials but it is a dynamite investment. Have at least 4-6 CDs for any given month. After every 6-8 songs place your ads or specials. This is a great way to advertise upcoming events. All of this can accomplished with a computer and and run seamlessly throughout the day and free your mind for important task. It makes the client feel like you're in the know so they are in the know. Put speakers throughout the salon area so that the music isn't blasting from one direction. The TV should be on something related to your business and should only be located in the reception area unless it features different products and services you offer. The main purpose of this is to entertain/educate the client, not you. Make a CD of your work, products you use, or interesting facts about hair, skin, make up, etc, and have that play all day on loop. It's good to have 5-6 CDs available. Yes, even the television needs to earn a spot on your walls. This is all part of the service. You want the client to walk out more educated than when they walked in.

The all important YOU

Unlike the lawyer at the beginning of the chapter, you want to keep yourself together. Exercise clothes have no place in a place made for beauty except the gym. Never should it grace your frame during your working hours, not even on your feet. You can purchase a nice stylish comfortable shoe. You have to set the standard for beauty and it starts with your over all look. Your hair has to be your billboard, also your nails and skin. If you have no time to do your hair, pull it back neatly and make sure it's shiny and clean. It's good to have some good quality wigs on hand because some days your hair just can't act right. This will make you look more knowledgeable. Make up is a part of your daily routine as well a fragrance but because there are those that have allergies, it should only be worn on the center part of your neck in a very small amount. That way you will leave a pleasant hug and those allergic can't smell you. Keep mints or strips in your station because they can be discreetly used.   If your nail polish is chipped or cracked take it off and buff your nails. Be sure to have lotion for your hands to keep them healthy. Your hair, your skin, and your nails are the core of your look. Why would someone want to trust you or pay you top dollar if you are half put together. If you are not wearing a uniform, it's time for you to be really stylish. Never underestimate the power of a well pressed lab coat. The lab coat is considered an object of authority and you are an authority in your profession. Have the lab coat professionally pressed and have it engraved with your name and the name of the salon.   Have your clothing, including lab coat, tailored to fit your body and pressed very well. If you can work in heels, do it; but always keep some comfortable flat, rubber sole, basic, non athletic shoe in your station or in the back room for a quick change if needed. Be mindful of your conversation. You don't want to be overly involved in any gossip that may be going on or having any inappropriate subjects for consideration as it may offend some clients. You need to be warm and inviting but you also need to control the atmosphere. Let it be known for positive vibes and not the latest gossip. You want to give off a corporate professional vibe and look. This is a profession and should be treated with all dignity.

Are you in shape? Did you know that those destined to succeed are more health conscious than those who don't give their size much thought? I know this is a touchy subject but if you are overweight make it a goal to lose 1-2 pounds a week. When you care about yourself it make others care about you too. You want this to be portrayed to your clients. Make it a routine of starting or ending your day with a good brisk walk at least 3 times a week. This will lift your spirit and make you a more positive and happy person. Cut out sugary sodas or snacks and replace it with fruit or lemon water. Start a group or join a group for positive enforcement. In one year you will be remarkably happier and richer.

Make affirmations a part of your everyday routine. We will talk more about this later.

Speak positives into your life and set goals. It would be great for you to keep a journal so you can see a record of your changes. You will be so impressed with yourself in just 12 short months to see your growth.

You are your business so you will have to learn marketing and re-booking later in the book.

You are the captain of your business so don't be afraid to be the leader you were meant to be. When you design your life in this way, success is inevitable. Remember that clients are looking for more and you have to set yourself apart from others. With a little practice this will become second nature and you will reap the benefits of having more money. This is designed to make you a package that will set the bar higher and makes it easier to charge what YOU are worth because you will not be competition on any level and you won't have to haggle with your prices. You will do the knock out service that is discussed later in the book.

All of this goes into the look. The look is all about marketing and subtle ways of enlightening and educating the client on what they want. Clients want to be serviced and that's what this look is all about. When you educate your clients in this way, they are automatically sold. A sold client will add dramatically to you overall ticket sale and profit margins and all you had to do was to look nice and to educate. It's that easy.

Just a side note...

You have to be in control of your environment by not allowing anyone selling things from food to puppies inside the salon. This should never happen. Your clients are paying for your time and the experience of your environment. Don't gossip around or to your clients. If there is any type of disagreement among the stylists, NEVER should it be handled on the floor. NEVER.

4. Have the "IT Factor" Personality

Focus, what is it? Focus is when you have your goals down and you are driven for success.

I have heard some people say "Well, this is just the way I am" as if that excuses you from bad or ignorant behavior. There is no place for that type of attitude in our business. To have an attitude that's not a positive one is to not have your focus. Everything around you can make you lose it. We live in a world that's designed to make you lose focus and crush your dreams. It can come in a lot of forms especially in the form of people. If you are a Bible reader you can recall the servant Job and his so-called comforters that told him to curse God and die... Wow, and they considered themselves friends of Job. I would hate to have them as enemies if they thought this was friendly. Today we call these people dream snatchers and they come in all shapes, sizes, and colors. Some of them will come from your own household or circle. You can't expect for everyone to be happy for you. You need to have two kinds of focus here.

Focus #1 is to focus on your goals that you have written down. Picture yourself there already. Spend some time each day measuring your path and how much you have accomplished in the journey. Focus on your freedom. Be it mental freedom or financial freedom. Feel that feeling in your head and body because this is how it becomes real. Freedom starts in the mind first.

Focus #2 is how you react to the things around you. Imagine you're in the salon. Your mood is good and your goals are on track. You just finished a knock out hair cut when the client begins to go ballistic about it being cut too short. You could say I can't do this and down yourself as not being that talented. You could let this person throw you off your game. This is where you, Stop! Redirect your focus. What was her mood like when she walked in the door? Refocus because she is not worth your whole day. Be happy and let positive-ness flow because this is where your creativity lies. Nothing can grow in a negative environment. Redirect by focusing on where you want to be. Listen to those that are moving in a positive direction and follow their advice and example. Remember to listen to positive and motivational CDs. Say affirmations every day and visualize those things happening. Redirect and drown that negativity out of your life.

Life is like a theater and the people around you are like an audience watching your life unfold. There are some people who don't deserve to sit on your front row. They may not be strong enough to watch or help you succeed and cheer you on. Be very selective as to who you allow to have a choice space in your life.

You must be the change you wish to see in the world -Mahatma Gandhi

Getting real with keeping it real

This will be a small section but will impact your life more than any other habit combined. I have heard the saying as well as you "I'm just keeping it real". Well, guess what? Keeping it real will keep you broke and that's "just keeping it real". Some people use this term and take this term way too loosely. Let me tell you what it really means... I have not taken the time to learn proper etiquette nor do I know how because I am really mentally lazy and I don't want to take the time to change. So I will just hide behind my bad behavior and hope I can fool you into doing the same... Don't do this. We ARE the "image business people" and we don't want to do things that would cost us growth, personally and business wise. We want to always be in a mindset of growth. Changing just this one thing can start a change in your clientele and when your clientele improves, so will your income. Not all clientele is good clientele. Not saying they are not good people but some clients will stay too long and want too much stuff that they can't pay for and you don't need that. Release the fear of change and move forward in a positive direction. You have to make success a habit.

Aristole said it best " We are what we repeatedly do. Excellence, therefore is not an act but a habit".

Act to change and change your act...

Keeping religion out of the workplace

I have passed by several businesses with religious sounding names. It's not just hair salons because I have seen yard services, repair men, moving companies, nurseries, you name it and people will put a religious sounding name on the business. I guess people think this is a way to give back to God. There is a problem here. We have to remember that this is your faith and not that of your clients. Clients come to you to get away from the hustle and bustle of their lives, not to learn about you. They are interested in what will make them better and not what's going on in your world. People come from all walks of life and they are going to patron businesses that make them feel welcomed and gospel music or religious sounding titles will isolate half of the people that would come to you for service. All of this is okay if you're planning on being a small operation without any substantial income, but if you're planning on making a serious living with this keep religion at bay unless you're asked and then it's not to be discussed where it can be heard all over the salon. As stylist we sometimes forget that this is an experience for the client. The client doesn't care if you 'Love the Lord' or if you go to the Big Mega Church down the street. They care about their hair, their experience, and how fast can you move so they can get on with their lives. Don't get overly familiar with your clients because you have to make a living and putting religion in your workspace can make you become too familiar. It's about money, not friends.

Finding a Mentor

If you wanted to be a doctor, would you hang out with a mechanic? The point is you have to have people around that you can admire because they are doing what it is you would like to do. Find successful stylist in your area and spend time with them. Join forums online with other successful stylist. I know you have heard the saying "Birds of a feather flock together." Look at your circle of friends and evaluate who it is you are hanging with. If you are the smartest, you need to reevaluate your relationship with these particular friends. I'm not saying dump your friends but do add some positive ones. When you start your transformation some of your friends will fall off because you no longer have the same mindset. Mentors are the most valuable players on your team. Your mentors have been where you are and they know where you're going. Having a mentor is like having a friend, a trainer, a teacher, a parent, a coach, a critic, and a cheerleader all in one. You can find them online, hair shows, business classes, or even look for stylist in your area that you would want to emulate. You can find some really good CDs with great mentors on them like Les Brown, Zig Ziglar, Kyle Cease just name a few. When you find a great mentor, tell them the truth about yourself so you can be helped to greatness yourself. Don't play games with a truly good mentor because you want to learn and soak up as much help as you can hold. You may have to kiss a lot of frogs before you find the one for you but that's okay because the point is you want to get real about yourself and be precise in your goals so that you can know where you are and where you're going. It takes a humble person to listen. You don't want to miss out on something great because you were talking so much that you talked yourself out of something or be so cocky that you're not teachable. I found several types of mentors because I had so many different needs and you may find yourself being the same way and that's okay, too. Get what you need.

5. Study your craft for the "IT Factor"

As stylist we have to stay on top of our craft. We are in a business that is ever changing. I have known stylists that don't keep up with education and give some of the most dated looks and you don't want that to be you. There is so much to this industry that we can learn more than we would ever need to know. We can't be good at everything so we need to decide what it is that we are going to be good at and study that. If you are good at styling, then study styles and directions. Like I said we are all not good at everything. This will also make you a specialist in the area you've chosen and specialist always charge more because they have dedicated their careers to knowing this one particular thing well. Read as much as you can in your chosen niche. Always have mannequins for practice and devote at least 3 hours a week to learning. I can't stress enough how much this will pay off for you in the long run.

Enjoy your craft. Brainstorm about it, do a fun photo shoot, write a blog, and articles about it. Post your work on your social network pages. Post everyday and really brand yourself with little sayings and keep things positive and inspiring. More on marketing later

Are you professional?

How you look, talk, write, act and work determine whether you are a professional or an amateur. There's really not enough emphasis placed on professionalism and how important it is to your success that people begin to think that being an amateur is normal.

A professional learn every aspect of the job. An amateur skips the learning process as much as possible.

A professional is focused and clear headed. An amateur is confused and distracted.

A professional does not let mistakes slide by. An amateur ignores or hide mistakes.

A professional is optimistic. An amateur gets upset and assumes the worst.

A professional helps the people around him. An amateur gossips about the people around them and sabotage their efforts for improvement.

A professional brings joy and solutions. An amateur brings negativity and problems.

A professional is a hero. An amateur is a victim.

Be a professional and go higher than you ever thought possible.

Keep up with continuous learning

I know you've known some stylists who try anything untrained and are quick to say they can do something that they know they can't. They are always looking for the cheapest way to learn something or what we will call bootleg an education. If you don't know this person... then maybe this person is you. Today learning is essential to your success. Specialize and take as many classes in the area you choose. Being a specialist will always get you exponentially more money than being a general stylist. Take as many classes as you can in your niche of the business. Set aside at least 3 hours or more a week to education and reading. Read things that motivate you too. We all can use a cheerleader in our corner to spur us on at times. Learn to love learning. Pour yourself into learning and you will began to love and you will be better at everything, personally and professionally.

Know your product

I know this was something that I was guilty of myself for years. I would use some of everybody's product line. I would use the relaxer from one line but the shampoo from something totally different. This is what I call being a product whore. There is no loyalty to no one and therefore if you had to explain it... You can't. We're quick to say I just like this and convert to the standard answer of I like the way this makes the hair feels.... But why? We don't know. Learning a product line is essential to your bottom line. 50% of your income is lost right here because we don't know enough to educate the client to sell them. Only use product lines that are willing to educate you for free and even give you the words you need to say to sell their products to your clients. You are becoming a frontline promoter for them and they should be willing to support you in that.

Keep it clean and in good repair

Pay attention to your area and your tools. Your tools should have no missing parts or cords that are taped or glued. Make sure your tools are clean. Clean tools will always look better and perform better than broken tools and it makes the client feel that you're giving them the best. Never use the same un-sanitized tools on the next client. Make sure your area is swept and clear of products on the floor or chair. Towels should be clean and never use dirty towels on clients. I have seen this done so that's why I had to mention. During my career, I worked in a salon that would run out of hot water quite often because the tank was too small for the amount of clients that came there. Rather than wait and put everything on hold in that area for 15 minutes, they would shampoo a client's hair in cold water! NO! This should never be done under any circumstance. It's so inconsiderate. Plan out your hot water needs and plan accordingly. Emergencies in a salon can happen at any time so it is a good idea to have a backup plan and practice it. Our job is to make sure the clients are safe and served. Plan it out Keep it safe. Keep it clean and keep it fun.

Speak well about your craft

Practice your speech so you can explain well what it is you do. Your pronunciation can make the difference in the type of salon you will be able to work in. Always look to improve yourself because you are more than worth the effort. Expand your vocabulary everyday and become a reader if you have not already done so.

Say daily affirmations

Speak well of yourself and others without being cocky

Compliment before being critical

Compliment at least 3 people a day

Life is like a mirror, what you put out will be reflected back to you.

6. Do the "IT Factor" Marketing

In a day how many times do you think of Facebook or go on there? Probably more than you think. Facebook is one of the biggest social media networks around and you need to be on it promoting your business. Now add Twitter, email marketing, and my favorite Instagram and you are ready for big things to happen.

If you are spending hours on FB a day you should definitely be advertising your business. Don't be so blatantly obvious with it. Do it in a more subtle way because people like to be a part of your life and not feel that they are being sold every time they read your post. Those types of post will eventually get ignored. There are a few ways to make money on FB but not in a straight obvious way. Here are a few ways.

1. Add friends and friends of friends but no more the 10-15 in a day so as not to send up red flags that you

are a spammer. Don't take FB too personal. I have come across people who won't add friends because they don't know them. In business that is suicide. Add as many friends as you can because that gives you free exposure and when your post pops up on their wall it becomes visible to their friends and that's more exposure for your talent. This is creating a worm hole for you to be seen by a wider market. FB is for your business not your personal. Get that part straight. Join groups of people with your like interest. This opens up a good opportunity to network and it exposes you to members as well as lookers. Post your parties, your creative styles, some everyday living and places. This will make you look alive and informative.

2. Post videos of your work or post a how to video. Don't make it so obvious that your advertising because no one likes to be sold. Post and ask a question like: What do you think of this style or color or you fill in the blank. This will get people to start talking about you. Put a link at the bottom of post so the person can find your web page or more of you videos or blog. Interact with people about things surrounding beauty and get opinions. Have surveys and contest that offer free prizes of some kind. Free things will always cause a buzz.

3. Brand yourself with a saying. I personally am known for 'ROCKING THE BOX'. Get something that can represent you and brand yourself with it and with good service. Be known for good vibes. You will quickly find out that the people you want will run to the positive and you want that to be you. Be known for the good feelings and positive thoughts but don't be fake. People like happy not phony.

Another good form of advertising is Instagram. It's a good sidekick for FB because the same thing you post on FB can be posted on your Instagram. Instagram is a good place to post on when your life is on the move. Do a photo shoot away from the salon and you can document the journey as well as the shoot. It would be like a day in the life of you. You can do the same with Twitter. Spend at least 15-30 minutes each day just on your business and social media sources. Document your journey as a stylist.

There are programs and apps available now that can help you save your time for other things. Saving your time is your ultimate goal. Some great apps that are so helpful with this are:

- DropBox- This is great for saving photos
- Trello- for projects and ideas
- Exchange

- One Password
- Shareweb
- Amazon Prime

All of these are designed to help you automate some of your day. Play around with some of these and see how they fit into your life.

Time is what we want most but what we use worst
- William Penn

Websites, newsletters and business cards

In today's world a website is essential to growth. You can get a free one if need be but you have to have one. Post your work and your happy face. Be knowledgeable and share some free hair tips and a special that changes often so traffic is driven there to check it out. Share it with your clients with some incentive to them for going there or booking there and sharing it with their friends. Post your blogs or hair tips that can be downloaded in exchange for their email addresses. This will build you a following that you are going to advertise to. Give gifts or dollar amounts off when they share with someone who comes in for a service. A good website can be so profitable and fun if you take some time with it. Post a newsletter that talks about trends or fashions. You know what your clients are into so you would want to tap into that. Offer exclusives only on your site to get your clients excited about the next giveaway like a printable coupon for something they can only get from you. Be your own model and have a contest online about maybe what was different about you today like maybe your hair color, lipstick (of course a color that only comes from you) or clothing, shampoo or whatever. I am making a whole course for marketing yourself in the salon because it's so much to it that it has to be separated so you can really benefit. Some good places to go to are:

www.godaddy.com good place for domain names and web design

www.webs.com reasonably price websites

www.vagaro.com and www.styleseat.com good websites and online booking

www.vistaprint.com for cards and all types of marketing material. They are also a good source for a website.

www.zazzle.com I really like their designs. Very different.

www.blogger.com is a another good place to start blogging. It's very user friendly and a good way to start for a beginner.

www.constantcontact.com is a good source for email marketing and sending out salon newsletters

Make sure to have business cards at all times because you never know who you're going to meet. You can also go to Office Depot for a basic business card if you just don't have any. They have a fast turn around (Less than a day) for basic black and white cards. Make sure your cards are in good repair without any of these BUSINESS CARDS NO NO's

No Dirty Cards

Outdated Cards

Bent cards

Clip Art Cards

The free cards from Vistaprint

Inked in phone number and names with the old info scratched out

BUSINESS CARDS Dos

Up to date photos of yourself or your work

Easy to read colors

Unique Designs that is uncluttered

Tell what you do or specialize in

Make your cards a standard size so they will fit into a wallet easily

Make your cards unique

Take up the front and the back of your card

I personally made my cards fun. Here's a sample of what my business card looks like. Front and back.

They were always a source of fun for any person I gave them to and they also became the conversation starter and I was able to help my prospect to see the value of what I was offering. It's also a card that won't so easily end up in the trash because of the perceived value attached to money. These were a lot of fun and they generated a lot of business.

Word of mouth marketing, Loyalty programs, Salon memberships, and other stuff

Word of mouth marketing will always be your best marketing by and large because it's cheaper and the person referred to you already has a certain amount of trust in you before they even meet you. Make your clients market for you even if they didn't want to. You can do this by offering a monetary discount for all referrals or let them offer gifts to those they choose to give a gift to. A good time for type of marketing is the Christmas season. Let them offer your services as stocking stuffers. Do this by having gift cards made with a monetary value on them 10.00 or 20.00 increments to spend on anything but retail. This will expose you to more of their friends and it makes your client looks as though they spent the money on the person. This is a win-win situation for you and them. You have parties that your client can invite their friend to. Parties designed to learn things about their hair, makeup, weight and the like but no specific brands or names. This goes back to being sold. No one likes being sold. Have thing available for purchase but have things they can't just go pick up at the local store or representative. Get things that are rare or exclusive like a local soap or perfume maker. Start your own make up line so that your colors are exclusive or pick a line with vibrant colors. You are an artist so market yourself as one and that makes people talk. You know beauty or we should. Just writing this makes me happy for you because this will change your life and make you think outside the box.

Loyalty Program cards are the best. They are cost effective and clients do like to see their circles pile up. There are some electronic programs that you can subscribe to and get the same thing. Vagaro and Styleseat both offer electronic ones with their services and a whole lot more.

Put a Membership plan in place that will allow your clients to pay you monthly via EFT. Members can have their services done for the month at a discounted price for paying all at once. Your can limit the amount of memberships you have available so scarcity is always in play and your membership stays full. I use memberships to cover my monthly expenses. That way my bills are taken care of for the month and the money is taken by EFT so it's always available to me on the first of every month.

Memberships have to have an application with a start and ending date as well as policies in place to protect your investment. Policies need to cover: Cancellations, freezing accounts, refunds, member transfers, insufficient funds, black out dates and times, fees...etc . Clients can commit to 3, 6, or 12 months. This is the best way to guarantee your income for a chosen amount of months or even years. Make sure that the client understands everything so there will be no surprises.

Some of the benefits of a membership are:

You know each month what your bottom line dollar amount is even if the client don't show up

Clients stay longer because they are committed

Clients have the ease of knowing every time how much the bill is

Money changes hand only once a month

Make a private VIP newsletter just for those in the membership that offers free things like lunch, products and educational parties. This will start your clients talking because they all want to be a VIP. You can price your membership fee to include all of the little extras.

Are you accepting Credit cards? If not it's time to change. There are several companies that are a good start for a small business and the cost is minimal. Some of them are:

www.sqaureup.com   They have an open market that can be seen by potential clients that are in the area. They also have a online store for your use. There fees are high but the transaction is completed when you swipe. Their swiper is free and fits well on cell phone and tablets. Great for a small business. I have used them for a number of years now.

www.paypal.com   Paypal opens up a whole new kind of market. Their fees are a little less than square and their swiper is free also. There is so many facets to Paypal that it would be best to visit their webpage for all of the details. I do like the fact that they pay quickly. It's usually within 15 minutes and you have your money.

A few others are:

www.swiperly.com

www.intuit.com

You can also do a merchant account if you have the volume of clients coming in. It does come with a monthly fee, contract, and equipment. I have done this too and it works just fine.

Get a business journal to help you keep up with everything related to your business. All you need is a spiral notebook and write down everything that you like and things that you need to know. Date your pages before you write your goals for the day down. That will help jar your memory about certain things. Sometimes we can remember the date or day that you had an amazing idea, but can't remember the idea. Thanks to your journal you can find it!

7. Do the "It Factor" knock out service

Our intentions is not to satisfy the client nor is it our intentions to please the client. Our intentions is to amaze them
-unknown

Stay focus on the experience

There is nothing more sacred to another person than themselves, so your focus needs to be on them. From the time the client walks in the salon greet them. If you're not ready for their service to begin always offer them a beverage and give them an estimate of time. If there is a receptionist make sure she offers them a beverage and tell them of your latest specials and what's available in retail. Take away all outdated, torn, ripped, and stained magazines. Do not let a client wait more than 10 minutes for her service to start or no wait at all. This can make her feel value her time. Sometimes we need to buy time and you should have certain procedures in place to cover you for that. You can also offer certain conditioning treatments for free if your time gets to be way off. An assistant is always a good investment and can help you stay on track with your time and help with making the experience a great one each and every time your client comes in. It would be a good investment to have the client change into a smock so that her clothes are protected and give her that choice to change. It should not be mandatory. No matter if this is her 1st visit or her 101th visit, always starts the service with an assessment of her needs. This should be done each and every time and can be accomplished in 3 easy questions.

What do you like most about your hair? / How was your hair this past week?

What do you like least about your hair? / Anything you liked least or best?

If you could get your hair anyway you want it, what would that be?

Listen carefully to the answers and so you know you understand then repeat it back at you heard to her in your own words for clarity.

After you have an understanding ask her if she would like your professional opinion of her hair. By asking if she wants you professional opinion has just established you as a professional in her mind and that's what you want. A client that sees you as a professional will be more loyal than one that sees you as just someone who 'washes' or 'do' her hair. This is the beginning of trust and people that trust you will spend more money and stay with you no matter where you go. If she is an established client you still want to know about her but you need to be creative so as not to sound robotic.

When shampooing, incorporate a small neck massage or have your assistant to do it. Set a timer so that you don't go over 5 minutes because #1 you have other clients to service and #2 you can't afford for her to get so relaxed that she slows you down. Time is still money but you want the experience to be memorable for her. Be sure to ask the questions because these questions are also designed to assist you with your retail sales so always follow through. Your client will be sold and sold on you and you did nothing but service her. When you service your client in this way, your prices will hardly ever come up but do be upfront about any prices and add-ons. Sticker shock can also drive clients away so be upfront.

Always collect client information from every client. This is the beginning of your marketing list. Remember you are about making an extraordinary living but it all comes from collecting information, marketing on those clients, and treating your clients with care and dignity. This is your beginning of SERVICING THE CLIENT.

Sometimes you may feel that you're asking too much but the client doesn't feel that way. The more you know the better you can serve them, so relax. I have a sample of a client profile sheet in the appendix for your usage. Now let's get into the little touches...

The little touches

This is where every person that comes into your space should feel special. You can be the best stylist in town but if you don't know how to treat your clients you won't have them long. It's the small things that will really take your service over the top. I will give you just a few things that will help you to take your service to another level. Here are a few here that will get you started and you will be well on your way to doing more and making more.

Greeting a client is so important. Smile, eye contact, and communication are essential for the comfort of the client. You want them to feel welcomed and this is your first step.

Smile- a smile cost you nothing but can mean the world to a potential client. Having a friendly face tells the client that you are open and ready for them. It displays a confidence that the client is in the right place.

Eye contact- eye contact tells the client that you see them and that they are important enough to look at. Don't just stare them down because that can get almost psycho feeling and that's not good. This is where men have to be careful. Make friendly eye contact and glance at her hair often so that she will know you're interested in her hair and not her. Give a comfortable and open look that says you are listening and not I'm crazy.

Communication- say something and let it be nice. If she has nice eyes say; your eyes are beautiful, I can make them pop with this or that cut, color, or whatever. Talk about the weather outside or the latest trends in hair and makeup. Be engaging and friendly.

REMEMBER

This will only take a S.E.C.ond. Smile - Eye contact - Communication. This acronym will help you to remember this and be open and friendly but not too personable.

If you have an assistant, you still make sure to take the time to speak to each and every client. This shows concern for them as well as sets the tone for the client to feel they are the most important person in the world at that moment.

It's good to invest or make gift or welcoming packages for you new clients. Don't forget your seasoned clients. Even though they are familiar with you and the salon doesn't mean that they should not be treated special.

Buy luxury towels- make sure they are clean and of good quality.

Have a beverage/snack bar- Always offer something to drink and make sure it's well stocked. This is something that is already added into the price of you service.

Have salon information available- Salon information should include brochures on products, articles on hair and hair services, specials for the month, newsletters that you write, your retail news, what's new and hot, new services and contest being offered or coming soon, and anything else that makes you forward moving.

Keep things clean- capes, smocks, towels, tools, and surroundings. Have blankets and step stools for dryer time.

Know your stuff

I can't stress enough to know your craft. Don't pretend to know something and you mess up. Anything that you do with hair, be trained in it. Spend the money for education. It's tax deductible so why not. Having the training and education builds confidence in you. It also teaches you how to sell the service or the product.

"The more that you read, the more things you will know. The more that you learn, the more places you'll go."
— Dr. Seuss, I Can Read With My Eyes Shut!

Watch your mouth

Many things can be said in a salon but when the conversation leads to gossip, you don't want to participate. We all talk. That's human nature but your job is not the place. There is salon talk and then there's kitchen table talk. Don't confuse the two. Never down another stylist or her work to a client, even if she is not a stylist in your salon. That's wrong and catty behavior and will come back to bite you in the butt if you do. Gossip can tarnish your professionalism, makes you look petty, and makes you lose clients that don't want to be around that. Just, don't do it.

"Great minds discuss ideas. Average minds discuss events. Small minds discuss people."
— Eleanor Roosevelt

8. Sell the "IT Factor" Retail

I understand if this subject can make a lot of people uncomfortable because you don't want to be pushy or demanding to your client but I'm going to show you here that it does not have to be that way. You can sell your client without coming across as pushy or desperate. We have to get into the mind set to making money more than just one way. Retailing can add 1000's to your bottom line by the end of a year and who can't use some extra funds. Understanding your product is key and having just 1-2 product lines that you use will come in handy. I would suggest that you only use professional products and those that offer training classes. The reason why is because this is where you will learn the language to sell. You need to be able to explain any product you use and carry. Everything in this section goes hand in hand so read through it carefully and in order to get the best impact.

Educate to sell

Education is not only key for you but also for your client. You cannot be afraid to educate your client. The more services you can offer one client the more it's likely you will retain that client for a while. When a new client comes to you, she is putting her trust in you and you should not disappoint. Educating your client should always start with a consultation with the client. Your consultation always starts with the questions mentioned in an earlier chapter but I will put them here for emphasis. They are:

What do you like most about your hair? / How did you hair do the past week?

What do you like least about your hair? / Anything you liked least or best?

If you could get your hair anyway you want it, what would that be?

The later questions are for you repeat clients. You always want to show concern for all clients and this will give them a special feeling about you and their service by you. Whether it's their first visit or their fifty-first visit you don't want to get overly familiar that you forget to treat them with the professionalism they deserve.

Listen carefully to the responses to the questions so that you can repeat the answers back to them in your own words. After you have clarity of their needs, say;

I understand. Can I offer my professional recommendation?

This question will set you apart as the professional you really are. You will begin with telling them what they asked for and what you would recommend.

Example text may go like this:

I understand that you like the color of your hair and the thickness but you would like for it to frame your face better and you would like more shine. I understand. Would you like my professional recommendation?

Client: yes

Stylist: I love the color of your hair also and it goes so well with your skin tones. Your eyes are so pretty and we want to make them pop by putting some highlights around the face and do an all over hair glace to enhance your color and let's add a fringe bang to really soften your jaw line and bring out you smile. You have a nice shape face and beautiful skin and that would really open up your face and really open up your face and show off your natural glow.

Are you ready to get started? That question is your first step in asking for the sale.

I want you to notice that compliments are laced throughout the recommendation. This helps her to relax and feel better about herself and trust you have her best interest at heart. It makes her better able to hear and receive what you are saying.

Ask for the sell

Are you ready to get started? Is your first question into the introduction of asking for the sale? At this point you have added about 2-3 extra services and she may have come in for just a hair cut. When you ask for the sale you don't want to mention price. Let the client be the first or you can say: would you like to have that itemized out for you to look at. Have a printout with all of your suggestions and the prices listed. It is a good idea to have a buy now price and a regular price so the client can see the value of doing it today. You're going to so the same thing with your retail products. You can ask the client: what would you like to start with today? Let the client tell you what they want.

Every product you use needs to be shared with the client as well as placed in their hands if it is a retail product. This would include the shampoo you use, the conditioner, creams, gels, or anything else that is a part of your retail line. You are going to demonstrate how the products are to be used and how often. You should educate the client so that they can repeat the look at home. This will make you look like the professional you are and it gives a confidence that your clients will admire and share with their friends. You are educating your client all the way through the service, by placing the products you used in front of them and explaining their usage, and you are helping the client to be able to style their hair like you styled it that day. All of this is putting together a package that the client can see.

Package it well

At the end of the service, all of the products that you use should be pulled and placed at the receptions desk; however it is not the job of the receptionist to complete your job at this moment. Once you have finish with the client, always walk the client to the front desk and show her all of the products you would recommend for her home care. You should offer between 3-5 products and this is what you say:

These are the products that I recommend for you today. What would you like to take with you today? This question is another 'asking for the sale' question. Have an all inclusive price like 20% off for all or 10% off of al la cart items that go home today. Once you have asked this question you are at this point to be quiet and say nothing as the client decides what it is they would like to purchase. After everything is said and done you always want to thank the client for allowing you to service them and ask what type of schedule will work for them because you are going to rebook them at this time and you should offer a discount on the next service for booking now.

9. Get the "IT Factor" Rebooking

With every client you should make it a point to get them to rebook. Clients don't know what to do and if left to decide on their own won't make a choice. 3 simple words need to become a part of every part of the experience. That is:

Call to Action

We all have a tendency to drag our feet on matters and your clients will do the same. Remember your goal is to fill your book and this is done by rebooking. A call to action is something that always has something that is a deal that's hard to pass up.

Offering the client a discount or something free like a deep conditioning treatment or partner with a manicurist for a day to offer mini manicures with the possibility of upsales. This will showcase a different service provider as well as make the client feel they are getting great value for their dollar. You can also offer a monetary discount or gift package that includes accessories; small products, etc. make it good and something that someone would want to have. This is where your wholesale license will come in handy. Spend about 10.00 per bag but you will put your retail value on the bag and make sure it's presented with your retail value. This is to be given with their next visit not now. Have pictures or a sample of what they will get upon their return. This is creating value to the client in a monetary way.

You would want your call to action to expire so as to create a feeling of urgency. You want that person on your book before they leave the salon and you would want to give them an appointment reminder card and thank them for their visit again. If you have a receptionist then at this point she can take over and you are free to move on to you next client.

This system will take practice if you are not use to retailing to your clients but practice will make this feel like second nature. You would want to practice this with every client because without doing the whole system of serving you are not giving your clients the best you have to offer and you are cutting your dollars short.

Always shop sales and wholesale to keep all kinds of things for gifts. Never spend more than what will be returned. It's good to offer sample products of things that you sale. Never put in things that can be found anywhere. Always partner with other talents locally for homemade soaps, oils, jewelry, hair DVDs that you make, etc. Have things that you can retail through your business. Keep it simple and fresh. That will give you another thing to retail if the client uses what's in their basket and loves it.

10. Bonus:
Get the "IT Factor" Credit Work on your credit

You're at work and the phone rings. You cheerfully answer the phone only to discover it's a debt collector. They are asking personal question and try engaging you in conversation. You're smiling and trying to be discreet. Embarrassing it is, but you have to grin and bear it or embarrass yourself even more by trying to excuse yourself so you can talk or hang up on them and everybody knows now so you have to act like nothing has happened. What to do? If you had the money you would take care of this and other things. Your credit is not only a way to move ahead but can really boost your self esteem. However, bad credit it not the end of your life and there is a way to get it paid. Here are a few rules to follow.

Rule # 1 Know your rights. You should make it a priority to know what a bill collector can and cannot do.

Don't guess and don't take the advice of people who are guess-ti-mating . You should know. Go to Fair debt collections and practices Act and Fair Debt Practices and read your rights first hand. It makes a difference.

Rule#2   Pull a copy of your credit report and know where you stand.   Know how to read it and what plan of action to take. More about this a little later

Rule#3   Stay off the phone. They Call. You hang up before you mess up. Know where you stand first.

Rule #4 Never, Never, Never Trust a debt collector.

Rule #5 If you get confused, refer back to rules# 3 and 4.

If your credit is slow or bad

All things are open for negotiating. A good place to visit is:

www.CREDITBOARDS.com That site is a wealth of information and will help you on the road to recovery.

www.BKforum.com   That's a really good site to find out as much as you can about bankruptcy.

Before you do anything to or with your credit, visit these sites first. Take it one day at a time and have a plan or make a plan.

You can get a free copy of your credit report every year. Make sure to get it from all 3.

Know your rights, you will find a link to them on the Credit Boards. The web address is above. Go there and read, read, and read.

You and your credit and money

Take good care of your credit. It can help you to buy the thing necessary for your business. Use your credit only for things that going to make you better or a profit. This goes for your money as well. Always save 10% of every dollar you make. That is yours to keep and it will go a long way later. That is a part of paying yourself first. DO NOT MISS THIS STEP!!! These are your seeds to your future. I cannot stress enough about the Creditboards website. The information is so vast and you will learn everything you need to know to start whatever today. Make a 1 year goal to be better than you are right now and map your process. This will be a big boost to your self esteem. It feels good to be free of that drama. You will see. Make good use of books. Learn about your credit, saving, and investing. Some really good books that I have read are:

Rich Dad, Poor Dad by Robert Kiosaki- I stumbled across this book many years ago now while hanging out in the book store and it has really served me well. I learned so much and it did change my thinking. I was so pumped after reading the first I read his entire series of books.

The Richest Man in Babylon- another great read. I learn the value of savings here.

Not only did I read those books, but I make it a practice to read something that will enhance my thinking and I suggest you do the same. The world looks so different when you learn.

I am not a credit expert but I know this is something that plagues most people at some time and point in our lives. I know I had to personally deal with it and I know how depressing it can be. I know for sure that if you take some time to educate yourself on where you are BEFORE you try and tackle it will make all the difference in the world to your credit, credit worthiness, and self-worth. Having bad credit also doesn't make you a bad person, contrary to what you may hear. Save yourself and stay off the phone and work out a strategy you can live with and complete. A ringing phone sounds like an emergency but it's not and whatever damage can be done to your credit report is pretty much done so you do what's best for you not them and work it out in your favor. Read before you pay!

11. Plan for your "IT Factor" future

Being a hair stylist can be a rewarding life if you take the time to learn the business side of it, but as time moves on and you get older how will you plan your future? Do you still want to stand behind your chair in 10, 20, or even 30 years or more? Would you like to transition into a salon owner if you haven't already? How will you do it and when? From here to the time you retire you need to set goals.

Set your goals

Think about all that you want to accomplish and the roadmap to get there. Make short term as well as long term goals. This is a good time to think about diversifying your sources of income. Things to think about are:

Would you like to do your own product line?

How many years can you sustain yourself standing behind your chair?

What is your plan B in case you are disabled?

What about your health and life benefits and/ or plans?

Will you diversify your funds into other business ventures or real estate?

These are just a few questions that you will need to answer and I'm sure you can think of more. Our time behind the chair can be shortened or lengthened depending on how you plan. Set your goals so you will know what it takes for you to sustain.

Achieve your goals in steps

Putting your goals down in steps will surely help you to accomplish them. Writing down your goals is a lot like planning a vacation or a trip. You first need to know:

Where do you want to go? Let's say you're planning a trip to New York. One of the first things you need to do is see how far it is from where you are. Next, you have to look at the different ways of going and choose the route that best suits your needs. Once you begin your road trip, you will make sure you're watching the markers and signs along the way that tells you that you're on the right track. In your mind you may have broken your trip up into milestones so you can see and feel your progress. Making your personal goals is much the same process. You decide how successful you want to be. Make a note of where you are and map out your plans to progress. Break it down into doable chunks so you can see and feel your progress.

The laws of attraction

This is one of the things I learned along the way. I was very doubtful at first but I gave it a try anyway. I don't know how many of you have seen the movie or read the book, <u>The Secret</u>. The concept of the secret is not new, but has been around for hundreds of years. When I discovered it, I began to use it when I thought about it with little success until I realized that I was limited by my own mind. Inside each of us is a giant, a creature, a designer of all things great. Recognizing that you have been blessed with a gift to ask the universe for anything and receiving it is one of the most liberating moments. I want you to know this and release your own power for greatness. The law of attraction is really a systematic approach to your goals. It's a process of knowing you deserve better and getting there. It's a changing of your mind and taking the limitations off your thinking. Write out what it is you want and go for it. If you shoot for the moon you may land on a star. Practice the art because that's what it is an art form. Don't give up but keep doing it. It will make you believe in yourself and your power. You are creating your life and your experiences and what you put out will be what you get back. You want it to be good things so you have to put out good things. Leave all negative talk about yourself and what's going on around you out of your life because you are like a magnet and you will attract those types of things. Let it go and find the positive. Be aware of your words. Stay away from negative words and thinking. The universe only understands things spoken in positive terms. The words "I am" are one of the most powerful terms you can say because you are or will be who you say you are. You are powerful, wonderful, and endowed with greatness. Control your thoughts, your actions, and your feelings for a greater and better you. The Secret really is not a secret, it's a practice. Be positive and be grateful as much as possible because a negative and a positive spirit can't dwell in the same vessel at the same time. When you realize that you are a walking, breathing magnet in your life is when you will be able to change your direction. Practice this and watch your life explode.

I hope this information was helpful to you and I hope you do and use a lot of the tips you have read. I know a lot of these tips are things that really have helped me to change my life and the way in which I worked. I am so thankful and grateful for all of my experiences because it made me who I am. I hope sincerely that this book blesses you with the life of your dreams. Be blessed.